For my tutor, friend and mentor, Martin, who also
illustrated this story, once upon a time ~ N.P.

First published 2005 by Walker Books Ltd,
87 Vauxhall Walk, London SE11 5HJ

2 4 6 8 10 9 7 5 3 1

© 2005 Niroot Puttapipat

This book has been typeset in Centaur and Linotype Zapfino

Printed in China

British Library Cataloguing in Publication Data: a catalogue record for this book is
available from the British Library

ISBN 1-84428-020-9

www.walkerbooks.co.uk

The Musicians of Bremen

A Brothers Grimm tale, retold and illustrated by

Niroot Puttapipat

WALKER BOOKS
AND SUBSIDIARIES
LONDON · BOSTON · SYDNEY · AUCKLAND

"Well, my friends," said Donkey as she approached the hearth, "what music shall we play this evening?"

"Monteverdi!" crowed Rooster from the footstool.

Dog circled a few times before settling on the hearthrug, saying, "No, let's play something by a German composer ~ Schütz, perhaps?"

"Why not something by a woman!" said Donkey, brightening, "Hildegard of Bingen!"

"If I may suggest ~ ," interrupted Cat silkily. The others turned to him. "Instead of making music tonight, why not let Donkey tell us a story ~ our favourite?"

There was a chorus of agreement as the others looked expectantly up at Donkey.

"All right," she said. Then, with a smile, she began. . .

For many years Donkey worked tirelessly for her master carrying sacks of flour and many others things to and from the mill and the market. But there came a time when she was becoming too old to bear the heavy loads.

"There's no money in that old donkey any more," said the master, "she'll have to go."

Donkey didn't like the sound of this at all, so she ran away.

"I shall go to Bremen to become a musician!" she brayed. "I will play the lute." Whom should she meet on the way but a forlorn-looking dog panting on the road. "Are you hurt?" she asked. The dog looked up dolefully and shook his head.

"I can't keep up with my master's hunting

pack as I used to. Because of this he plans to kill me!

I ran away and now haven't the heart to go any further."

"Then come with me!" cried Donkey. "We'll go to

Bremen and become town musicians. I can play

my lute and you can beat your kettledrum!"

Dog gave a gleeful bark and joined her.

Soon they met a miserable cat by the side of the road.

"Don't look so mournful," Donkey said, "whatever's the matter?"

"I'm not so very young any more," he sighed. "My teeth and

claws are not what they were and I am no longer so good

at catching mice, so my mistress means to drown me.

What am I to do now?"

"Come with us," replied Donkey. "We're going

to Bremen to make music and could

do with a good serenader like you!

Come and be the violinist to my

lutenist and Dog's drummer."

The cat was delighted. Now

a trio, they continued

on their way.

Before long they came across a rooster perched
on a farmyard gate. He looked
utterly furious and was
crowing for all he
was worth.

"Oh, dear," said Donkey,

"what can be so wrong?"

"What's wrong?!" wailed the rooster.

"Only that the mistress of the house

is preparing to wring my neck for

Sunday lunch, despite my

prediction of fine weather for

Our Lady's Day today! So now

I'm making all the noise I can

while I'm still alive!"

"Then put it to better use," Donkey replied, "and come with us to Bremen. I'm a lutenist, Dog's a drummer, Cat's a violinist; and with a voice like that you will make a fine tenor. We'll be the best troubadours the town has yet known!" The rooster loved the idea. He joined them, and as a new quartet they went together towards Bremen.

By nightfall they had arrived at a forest. Dog and Donkey settled down under a tree while Cat and Rooster took to the branches. From his perch at the top, Rooster could see a light from a distant house – this would certainly be a more welcome place of rest. They crept towards it and found it to be a little cottage. Donkey peered in through a window and saw what appeared to be a band of robbers.

"What else can you see?" urged the others.

"Why, there's a table groaning under the weight of good things to eat!" answered Donkey breathlessly. "Grapes and peas, puddings and pies, roasted meats and wine!"

Gasping with hunger, the animals put their

heads together and came up with a plan to seize

the cottage and its contents for themselves. First Donkey

stood with her hooves on the windowsill. Then Dog

jumped onto her neck. Cat pounced upon Dog's back

and Rooster flew up to perch on Cat's head.

At a signal from Donkey, they at once launched into their

music together and crashed in through the window. Donkey

brayed away the bass continuo, Dog drummed ferociously

with his barking, Cat provided counterpoint with the

miaowing of his violin whilst Rooster sang a

gloriously alarming aria! The robbers bolted

out of the cottage, terrified that a monster

had burst in, and ran into the woods.

$\mathcal{T}$*he musicians* gathered around the table and ate as though they'd never eat again. When every morsel was gone, they put out the light and found places to sleep.

Donkey took the pile of straw in the yard,

Dog lay down behind the door,

Cat curled up by the fireside

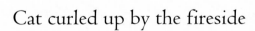

and Rooster flew

up into the rafters.

Meanwhile, the robbers
had been keeping watch
from the woods and the
chief soon sent one of his
men back for their loot. Finding the
cottage in darkness, the robber
decided to strike a light. Cat, crouched by the hearth,
regarded him warily. The robber mistook his glowing
eyes for live coals and held a candle close to them. What
impertinence! thought Cat, and he leapt up, spitting and
scratching the robber's face. With a cry, the man stumbled
towards the door, whereupon Dog jumped up and
sank his teeth into the robber's leg.

The terrified man ran screaming into the yard and
from there Donkey sent him off with an almighty kick.
As a finale, Rooster flew from the rafters to the top of
the cottage and cried: "Cock-a-doodle-doo!"
The robber shrieked, "Oh monstrous! Oh strange!

We are haunted!" as he staggered

away back to his gang.

The next day, the friends heard from a pair of pigeons a most delightful tale that had been circulating of robbers fleeing a cottage which was overrun by some truly terrifying beings.

One of the robbers had been scratched viciously by a dreadful witch, stabbed in the leg by a troll and then struck a merciless blow by a demon with a club. What was more, on the roof sat the devil himself, bellowing "Hell for you too!" as the man made his escape. It was said that the robbers vowed never to venture near the place again.

The four friends could not stop roaring with laughter!

"The robbers never did return,"

said Rooster with satisfaction.

"Nor did we ever make it to Bremen, after all," murmured Dog.

"The cottage is so much to our liking," purred Cat.

"So here we are," sighed Donkey happily, "making our wonderful

music together."

The German **Bremen Town Muscians,** included in the Brothers' Grimm second edition of their *Children's and Household Tales* in 1819, is probably the best-known version of this tale. Other variants include one from Switzerland, which features a horse instead of a donkey and a goose instead of a rooster. There is also an interesting version from mid-nineteenth century America, in which, like the Swiss tale, the animals are not musicians. Here, the adventure is started by the dog, who simply grows tired of his guarding duties. His reluctant companions are only persuaded to join him when he warns them of their fates when they grow old.

The closest version to the Grimms' tale comes from Flanders. The animals' intended destination is the Cathedral of St Gudule in Brussels, where they plan to become choristers (four *voices* rather than one voice and three instruments). In this tale they good-naturedly hope to be rewarded for singing and only accidentally fall in through the window – with satisfactory, if not quite the intended, results!

I have chosen to set my retelling in the early seventeenth century. This gave me the chance to have the animals mention a few great composers of the time and so strengthen the musical aspect of the story. Some retellings have the donkey's instrument as the horn – but I think the lute's sounds are more suited to a donkey's braying, as well as fitting in well with the music of the period.

The composers mentioned are: Claudio Monteverdi (1567–1643), Italian composer of operas and church music, and Heinrich Schütz (1585–1672), from Germany. The exception to these contemporaneous composers is Hildegard von Bingen (1098–1179), a German nun and composer of plainchant and sacred music. Donkey mentions her because of course she too is female. I thought it was high time this tale featured a female as the leader of the group!

Niroot Puttapipat

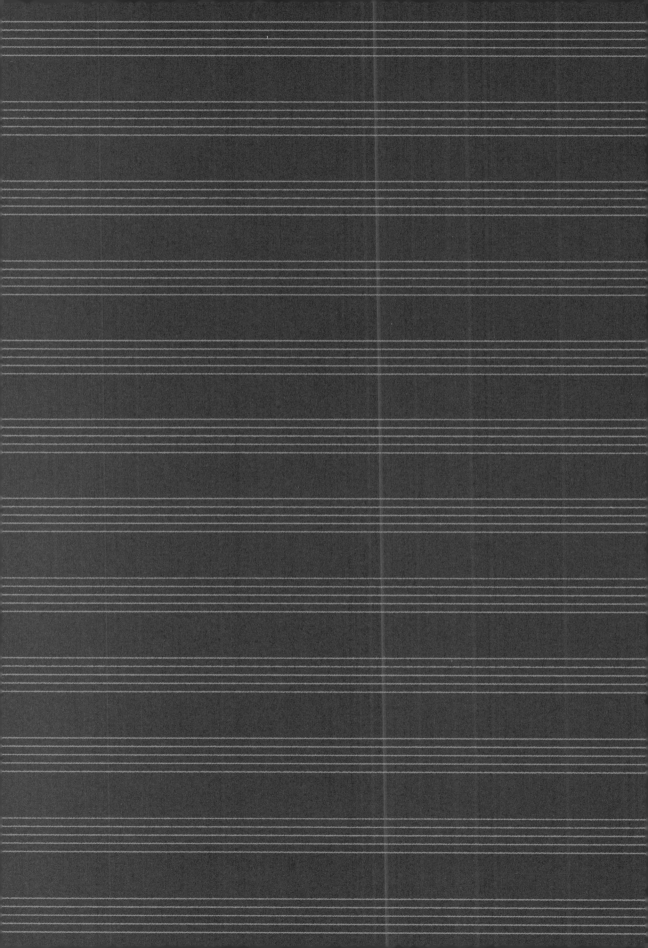